D0687322

Justin Morgan
and the Big Horse Race

By Ellen F. Feld
Illustrated by Jeanne Mellin

Willow Bend Publishing
Goshen, Massachusetts

To Jeanne—
I am truly grateful for all the amazing drawings
you've created for my books through the years.
Above all, I am blessed to call you 'friend,' and
I look forward to many more lively talks about
our beloved Morgan Horses!

Copyright © 2013 by Ellen F. Feld

All rights reserved, including the right of reproduction in whole or in part in any form.

Library of Congress Control Number: 2011945942
ISBN: 978-0-9831138-1-2

Illustrations by Jeanne Mellin
Book and cover design by Jennifer Conlan

Published by Willow Bend Publishing
P.O.Box 304
Goshen, MA 01032

www.willowbendpublishing.com

Printed in Korea

A long time ago, in the hills of Vermont, there lived a very beautiful horse. His body was brown, and his legs, mane, and tail were black. He had tiny ears and big, BIG eyes. He also had the longest, thickest mane and tail in all of Vermont. His name was Justin Morgan.

Justin Morgan worked very hard every day. In the spring, he plowed the fields so crops could be planted.

In the summer, he carried his owner through the woods, up and down hills, and in and out of streams. The beautiful horse even got hooked to a cart so he could have trotting races with some of the other horses who lived nearby.

In the fall, he was hitched to a work harness and
pulled huge, heavy logs out of the ground.

In the winter, Justin Morgan pulled a sleigh into town so his owner could buy supplies.

When Justin Morgan didn't have to work, he spent his time in a big field full of tall, tasty grass. He loved to eat the juicy grass as his tail swished away the flies. But his favorite thing to do in that field was to

RUN, RUN, RUN!

When Justin Morgan ran, he was very, very pretty with his long mane and tail blowing in the wind. The proud horse tossed his head around and jumped and snorted in glee. Animals from all over the pasture, the woods, and the mountains loved to watch the horse run. And Justin Morgan was so fast; he could outrun all the other horses in town.

Word of Justin Morgan's speed soon spread to other towns, and from there, to other places, far, far away. Was there any horse who could run faster?

One day, while Justin Morgan was grazing in his pasture, he noticed two new horses. Justin Morgan stopped eating and watched the two horses slowly make their way toward him.

The two horses were very different from Justin Morgan. While he was brown with a long, long mane and tail and short, sturdy legs for climbing the hills of Vermont, the two new horses had very thin manes and tails. Their bodies were tall and lean, and their legs were very long and slender. These horses were built for running FAST!

"My name is Sweepstakes," one of the horses said to Justin Morgan.

"And my name is Silvertail," said the other horse.

"I'm called Justin Morgan," replied the pretty brown horse from Vermont.

"We have traveled a great distance," explained Sweepstakes, "because we heard that there was a very fast racehorse living here. We are racehorses too, and no horse has ever beaten us. We want to race you!"

Justin Morgan knew he was fast. He knew he had never been beaten by the horses who lived nearby, but he had never run against a real racehorse. Could he win a race against two very fancy, very experienced racehorses?

"Where is your racetrack?" asked Silvertail.

"Racetrack?" replied Justin Morgan. "Racetrack? We don't have one."

"That's impossible!" insisted Sweepstakes. "Every town has a racetrack."

"Not here in the hills of Vermont," explained Justin Morgan.

"Then how do you race?" asked Silvertail.

Justin Morgan told his two new friends about the long dirt roads scattered all over town. "We race on the roads," he said. "We pick a starting point and a finish line and then we

RUN, RUN, RUN!

"Hmmmmm....." said Sweepstakes, "it is too far to go all the way back to New York to race on our track. I guess we'll have to race you on one of those long dirt roads."

The next day, all the animals in and around Vermont gathered along the sides of a dirt road just outside town. It was one of the few places where the road didn't go up, down, or all around a hill or mountain. It would be the perfect place for a race!

Justin Morgan was the first horse to arrive. He pranced and whinnied and tossed his head from side to side. He could not wait to race!

Soon the two other horses arrived. They slowly walked toward Justin Morgan, and then Sweepstakes said, "Silvertail will race you now."

"Just Silvertail?" asked Justin Morgan.

"Yes, just Silvertail."

Justin Morgan did not understand why Sweepstakes was not going to race, but because he wanted to run, he agreed and pranced over to the starting line. Silvertail followed the Vermont horse and stood quietly, with his hooves touching the white starting pole. Both horses looked over to the side of the road where a fuzzy, fluffy bunny shouted, "Ready, set, GO!"

Justin Morgan shot off like a bullet, his powerful back legs pushing him up and out, his front legs reaching far in front of him, grabbing at the dirt road. Silvertail flew into action too – his long, long legs reaching far beyond his chest.

"Go! Go! Go!" screamed the horses watching the race.

"RUN, RUN, RUN!"

And Justin Morgan

RAN, RAN, RAN!

Silvertail was fast, but he wasn't fast enough. As the two horses approached the end of the race, Justin Morgan got an extra burst of speed and crossed the finish line before Silvertail. Justin Morgan won the race!

Justin Morgan was very proud of himself. He pranced and snorted and tossed his head in delight. He was tired from the race, but he knew he had to return to the starting line to see all his friends. Silvertail congratulated the brown horse, and then, huffing and puffing, made his way back to the starting point too.

"You won! You won!" shouted Justin Morgan's friends. "Now you are the fastest horse in all of New England and New York too!"

"Not so fast," warned Sweepstakes. "Justin Morgan still has to race me."

"What?" asked Justin Morgan and all his friends.

"You still have to race me," repeated Sweepstakes.

"But you didn't say anything about running twice," protested Justin Morgan. "I'm tired. I need to rest."

"When we agreed to race, I said 'WE' would race you."

"But you didn't say I would have to run two races. I thought you meant I would race both of you at the same time."

Sweepstakes snorted. "I am sorry you did not understand me. If you are tired, you can give up and admit that I am the fastest horse." He knew Justin Morgan was tired and probably could not run another race. But he did not know about the brown horse's spirit. Justin Morgan would never give up!

"All right. I will race you," agreed Justin Morgan as he walked back to the starting line.

Sweepstakes smiled at Silvertail. The two racehorses were sure that Justin Morgan would lose the race.

Justin Morgan pawed the ground as he waited for the second race to start. He snorted, swished his tail, and tossed his head. Then the fuzzy, fluffy bunny shouted, "Ready, set, GO!"

As in the first race, Justin Morgan shot off right away. But this time, Sweepstakes took off just as fast. Both horses ran, ran, ran, fast, fast, fast. But Justin Morgan was getting tired. Could he keep up his fast pace and outrun Sweepstakes?

The horses were running nose to nose, faster than any horse had ever traveled along those long dirt roads. The finish line was fast approaching, and nobody could tell who would win. First Justin Morgan was in front, then Sweepstakes inched into first place, then Justin Morgan stretched into the lead. Soon the finish line was right in front of them. Who would win? Sweepstakes was in front, but then Justin Morgan's friends yelled, "Go! Go! Go!"

The roar of his friends' voices was just what Justin Morgan needed. He gave a loud grunt, stretched out his legs, and flew over the finish line seconds before Sweepstakes!

Justin Morgan won the race!

Did You Know?

Justin Morgan, the man (1747-1798), was a teacher and musician. He was also a horseman and farmer. Born in West Springfield, Massachusetts, he moved to Randolph, Vermont, in 1788.

Justin Morgan, the horse, was born in 1789. While his origins are not known, he was acquired by Justin Morgan as partial payment for a debt. Originally named "Figure," the horse soon gained fame in and around Vermont. "As Figure grew, his compact muscular body and stylish way of moving impressed many…His ability to out-walk, out-trot, out-run, and out-pull other horses was legendary." – American Morgan Horse Association

As Figure's fame increased, people began to refer to him as "Justin Morgan's horse," and that name was eventually shortened to "Justin Morgan." Today, all Morgans can trace their ancestry back to Figure, the first Morgan Horse.

Justin Morgan and the Big Horse Race is based on a true story. The tale is taken from events that took place in 1796 in Brookfield, Vermont, when Justin Morgan raced two New York "running horses" named Sweepstakes and Silvertail. Each September, this famous race is honored when Morgans and their owners gather on that same stretch of road, now known as "Morgan Mile," and race in harness and under saddle.